Preparatory Level
REPERTOIRE

Exploring Piano Classics

A Masterwork Method for the Developing Pianist

NANCY BACHUS

ISBN-10: 0-7390-5557-7
ISBN-13: 978-0-7390-5557-1

Alfred

About the *Exploring Piano Classics* Series

Exploring Piano Classics: A Masterworks Method for Developing Pianists pairs motivating performance repertoire with thoughtful technical studies. Each level contains two books:

- *Exploring Piano Classics—Repertoire* includes pieces from the major style periods. The repertoire was selected and graded by studying festival, competition, and examination lists from the United States, Canada, and the United Kingdom. Background information on each style period, its instruments, composers, and the music itself is included. The CD performances of the repertoire in each level provide an indispensable auditory learning tool for appropriate musical interpretation.

- *Exploring Piano Classics—Technique* includes **basic keyboard patterns**— five-finger patterns, scales, chords, cadences, and arpeggios in the major and minor keys found in the *Repertoire* book. These patterns can be developed into a daily warm-up routine for each practice session while expanding the student's technical skills. **Exercises and etudes**, an important feature of the *Technique* book, were chosen and written to develop basic keyboard touches and other necessary technical skills for mastering each piece. Suggestions for efficient practice are also included.

These companion books include a convenient page-by-page correlation, allowing the teacher to assign pages in the *Technique* book that reinforce the music that students are learning in the *Repertoire* book. When used together, the books give students a deep understanding of the art of music, performance practices, and the necessary skills to play the piano with technical ease. The knowledge, skills and joy experienced in the study of music through this series will enrich students throughout their lives.

CONTENTS

KEYBOARD INSTRUMENTS

During the Baroque and Classical Eras

The Baroque Era (1600–1750)

The term *Baroque* is used to describe a dramatic and very fancy style of art (paintings and sculpture), architecture (building designs), and music found in Europe around 1600 to 1750.

The Baroque Harpsichord

The **harpsichord,** often highly decorated, was the favorite keyboard instrument of the Baroque era.

Italian harpsichord, 1658
4 octaves

■ When a key went down, a quill moved up and plucked a string, so **dynamics** (loud and soft) could not be changed by the finger on the key.

■ Most harpsichords had one string for each note, but larger ones had two or three sets of strings and more than one keyboard (**manual**).

The Classical Era (1750–1820)

The term *Classical* is used to describe a style of European music from around 1750 to 1820 and to the art and architecture of ancient Greece and Rome, with emphasis on reasoning and use of the mind.

The quill plucking a string

The Pianoforte (Soft-Loud)

The **pianoforte** was actually invented during the late Baroque era (ca. 1700) by the Italian **Bartolomeo Cristofori** (1655-1731). However, this instrument was not widely played until around 1770, during the Classical era—the time period of the first true piano music.

Bartolomeo Cristofori

■ Cristofori called his invention a **harpsichord with piano and forte** (soft and loud). The name was shortened to **pianoforte** and then just **piano**. Modern replicas of late 18th-century instruments are called **fortepianos**.

■ When a key was moved, a hammer was thrown at the strings and fell back down, making it possible to play with a wide dynamic range.

■ Both the harpsichord and pianoforte were used in the Classical era.

Cristofori pianoforte, ca. 1720
4-4½ octaves

Walter fortepiano,
1792 (replica by Paul McNulty)
5½ octaves

During the Romantic and Modern Eras

The Romantic Era (1790–1910)

The term *Romantic* is used to describe 19th-century art, literary writing, and music. During this time, people became more accepting that feelings and imagination were important in learning and creating.

Pianos Grew Stronger in the Romantic Era

Around 1800, pianos became more popular than harpsichords. But when **Ludwig van Beethoven** (1770–1827) played, *"At the first chords of the solo, half a dozen strings broke"* on the delicate instrument.

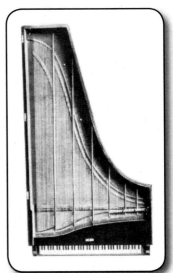

First "iron bar" grand piano, 1823
6 octaves

■ The wooden frame of early pianos would collapse if there were too many strings and they were pulled too tightly.

■ In the early 1800s, piano builders began to strengthen the frame by adding metal braces that could support the now 6-octave keyboard.

■ By the 1850s, the new all metal frame could support the longer 7¼-octave keyboard and its strings.

Romantic piano (mid-19th century)
7¼ octaves

Modern Era (1880–forward)

Around 1900, there were many different styles of music and art. Many artists painted ordinary people in their daily lives—working, boating, and dancing. Musicians became interested in the folk music of different cultures.

Pianos in the Modern Era

The inside construction of 20th-century pianos is about the same as in the late-Romantic era.

■ By 1890, 7¼ octaves were standard.

■ Concert grand pianos are approximately 9 feet long, and plain, black cases are favored.

20th-century piano
7¼ octaves

Use with *Exploring Piano Classics—Technique*, Preparatory Level
Warm-Up Patterns in G Major, pp. 6–8, Legato Touch, p. 9

BAROQUE

An Early Musical Instrument

Bagpipes existed more than 2,000 years ago at the time of ancient Greece and Rome.

- Tubes, called **pipes**, are inserted in an airtight bag, originally made from an animal skin.

- There are two kinds of pipes: the **melody pipe** or **chanter**, and the **harmony pipes** or **drones**. Drones usually sound the interval of a fifth, like the left hand of this piece.

- The pipes have a reed attached, creating sound as the air passes through it. (The air in the bag keeps the sound playing while the bagpiper breathes.)

- Bagpipes often accompanied dancing during the Baroque era and were used by people from all levels of society.

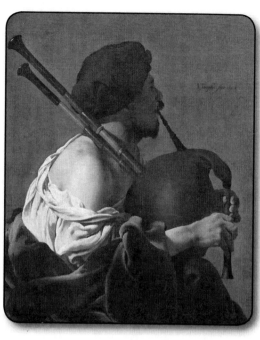

The Bagpiper (1624)

Bagpipe

Track 1

① (CD icon)

Anonymous

Keyboard Lessons in the 18th Century

During the Classical era, **the more scientific way of looking at life influenced music teaching.** Some teachers wrote detailed, almost scientific, books on how to play keyboard instruments.

- In 1789, the German teacher and composer **Daniel Gottlob Türk** published *School of Keyboard Playing,* which was used by many teachers.

- He wrote titles that would help students understand the mood of the pieces and encourage them to feel and show the emotions of music.

The Music Lesson
by Jean Carolus (1867–1880)

CLASSICAL

Beginnings Are Difficult

Track 2

Daniel Gottlob Türk
(1750–1813)

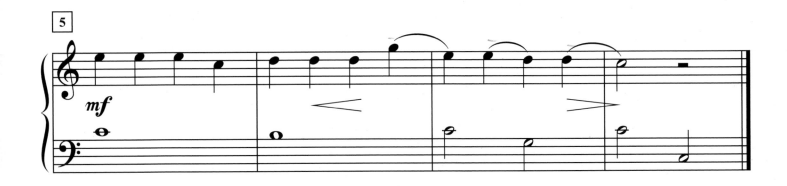

Warm-Up Patterns in G Major, pp. 6–8, Changing Tone Quality and Volume, p. 12, Slurs of Three or More Notes, p. 14

Baroque Dances

Almost all royal celebrations during the Baroque era involved dancing. These dances had many different rhythmic patterns and moods, as well as a variety of dance steps.

- **Philip Hainhofer** was a German art dealer in the 1600s who wrote a book about travel, and also composed music.

- His *Echo Dance* is very elegant, like the court dance pictured here. This dance has three musical ideas and each is repeated. In Baroque music, when a phrase is repeated, it is usually played softly the second time, like an **echo**.

Dance at Strasbourg, engraving
(Königlichen Almanach, 1682)

Echo Dance

Track 3

Philip Hainhofer
(1578–1647)

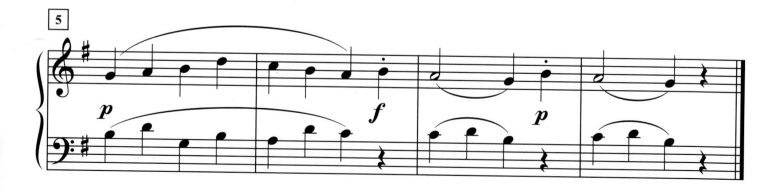

9

Warm-Up Patterns in C Major, pp. 6–8, Slurs of Three or More Notes, p. 14, Staccato Touch, p. 15, Slurs Ending with Staccato, p. 16

Music Lessons in the United States

Harpsichords and organs were brought to the United States from Europe in the early 1700s and **Thomas Jefferson** (1743-1826) ordered a piano from England for his new wife in 1771. Music and dancing lessons were popular in colonial America, but most teachers and music came from Europe.

Alexander Reinagle, a well-known teacher and composer from Glasgow, Scotland, settled in Philadelphia around 1786 after the American Revolution.

- He was one of America's first professional pianists, insisting on playing a piano, not a harpsichord.

- Reinagle's *24 Short and Easy Pieces* were composed in Glasgow, but were re-published in the United States for teaching.

- Reinagle taught **George Washington's** (1732-1799) step-granddaughter and this piece was found at Washington's home in Mt. Vernon, Virginia.

Alexander Reinagle

CLASSICAL

Allegretto

No. 6 from *24 Short and Easy Pieces*

Track 4

4

Alexander Reinagle
(ca. 1756–1809)

Imitation

The famous German organist **Michael Praetorius** was one of the best-known musicians of his time. He traveled throughout the northern German states performing and giving advice on how to build organs.

- He wrote an important book describing all the musical instruments of his day that was also illustrated with woodcut images.

- He composed more than 300 dances as well as other music.

- In measures 6 and 7 of his *German Dance,* the right hand plays the same pattern of notes just played by the left hand in measures 5 and 6. This is known as **imitation**, and is frequently used by Baroque composers.

Michael Praetorius

BAROQUE

German Dance

Track 5

Michael Praetorius
(1571–1621)

Moderato

LH legato

Warm-Up Patterns in G Major, pp. 6–8, Slurs Ending with Staccato, p. 16, Imitation (with Slur Touch), p. 17

Bartók in his traveler's costume before his first trip to Transylvania to study their folk music

Béla Bartók

Béla Bartók was an important 20th-century composer, teacher, and concert pianist.

- He traveled to rural villages in Hungary and nearby countries asking old people to sing the songs they had learned in childhood. He recorded more than 6,000 tunes.

- This music influenced his compositions.

- When he was asked to compose pieces for teaching piano students, he decided to use folk tunes.

- He published 18 pieces in a set for beginning pianists called *First Term at the Piano*.

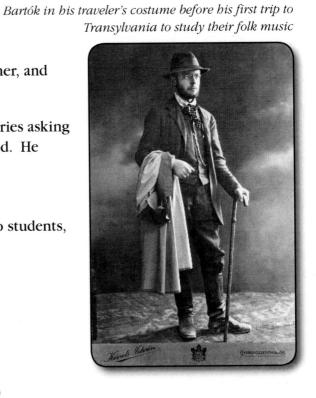

Moderato
No. 5 from *First Term at the Piano*

Béla Bartók
(1881–1945)

Track 6

6

MODERN

Keyboard Lessons in the 19th Century

During the Romantic era, the **Industrial Revolution** (when machines began to do man's work) affected music. Since musical instruments were often made in factories, they became less expensive and more people bought them.

- With more and better instruments available, many trained musicians became teachers and composed pieces for teaching.

- The German organist and teacher **Cornelius Gurlitt** is best known today for his hundreds of piano teaching pieces.

- Waltzes were very popular for dancing, for keyboard lessons, and to play on the piano for pleasure.

Cornelius Gurlitt

* Keep even speed throughout

Little Waltz

from *The First Steps of the Young Pianist*

ROMANTIC

Track 7

Cornelius Gurlitt (1820–1901)

Op. 82, No. 18

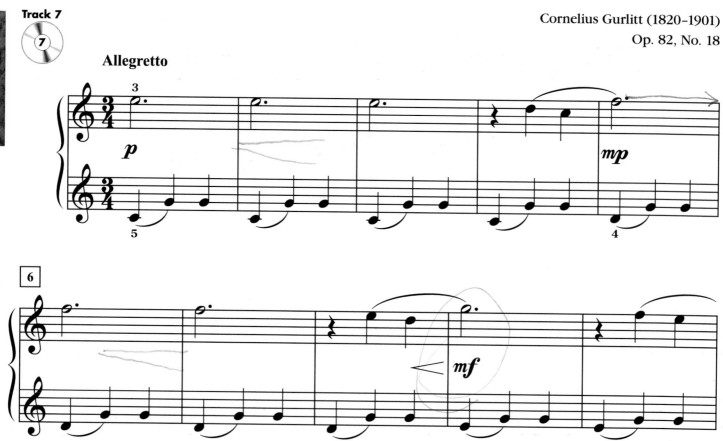

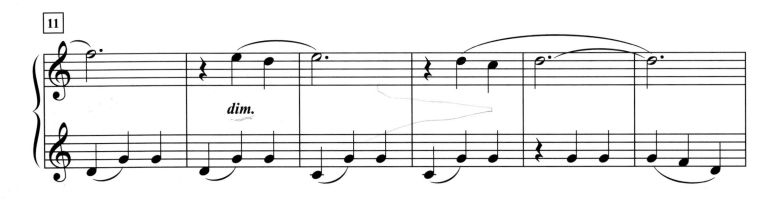

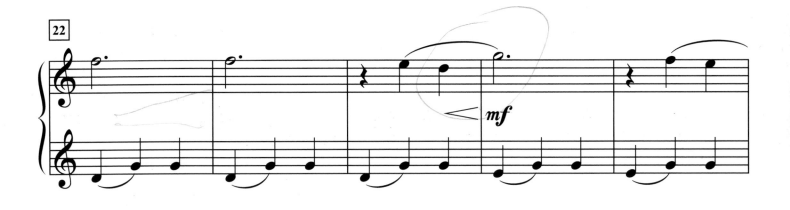

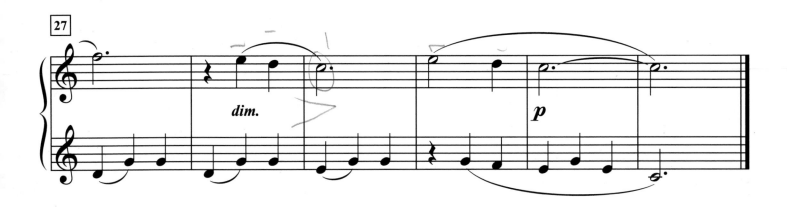

14

june 6

tenuto —

Warm-Up Patterns in F Major, pp. 19–20, More about Slurs, p. 21

Country Dances

Country dances developed in rural areas with couples dancing energetically in lines, circles, or squares. The next two pieces were written for students by the German piano teacher and composer **Heinrich Wohlfahrt**.

Track 8

Country Dance

Heinrich Wohlfahrt
(1797–1883)

ROMANTIC

Warm-Up Patterns in D Minor, pp. 22, 24–25

Romance for Piano

A **romance** is a melodic or song-like instrumental piece.
Shape the melody expressively.

Track 9

9

Romance

Heinrich Wohlfahrt
(1797–1883)

Andante con moto

ROMANTIC

Carl Czerny

Carl Czerny began studying piano with **Ludwig van Beethoven** (1770–1827) in Vienna, Austria, at the age of 10. Czerny later wrote and arranged 1,000 pieces for piano students.

Little Star is Czerny's arrangement of a well-known French folk song. Combined with a famous English nursery rhyme in 1806, this melody became widely known as *Twinkle, Twinkle, Little Star.*

Track 10

Little Star

No. 10 from *First Instruction in Piano Playing*

Carl Czerny
(1791–1857)

Warm-Up Patterns in A Minor, pp. 23–25, Consecutive Thirds, p. 28

Hungarian Folk Dance

Folk dances are usually performed by people with few or no dance lessons and reflect their culture.
Béla Bartók's folk dances were based on actual themes and rhythms that he collected in his travels.
He did not give this piece a title.

Track 11
(11)

Folk Dance

No. 6 from *First Term at the Piano*

Béla Bartók
(1881-1945)

MODERN

18

Program Music

The purpose of program music is to create a picture in the mind of the listener, often suggested by the title.

The term **shepherd pipe** has two meanings:

- A pipe is a hollow tube. This word is used to describe any tube-shaped wind instrument, but it usually refers to recorders or **flute-like instruments**.

- The other meaning is a **small bagpipe**. Either one suggests a shepherd alone with his sheep playing a rather sad song.

Shepherd with Flock of Sheep
by Niko Pirosmanishvilli (1863–1918)

Track 12

The Shepherd Pipes

Tat'iana Salutrinskaya
(dates unknown)

Andante cantabile

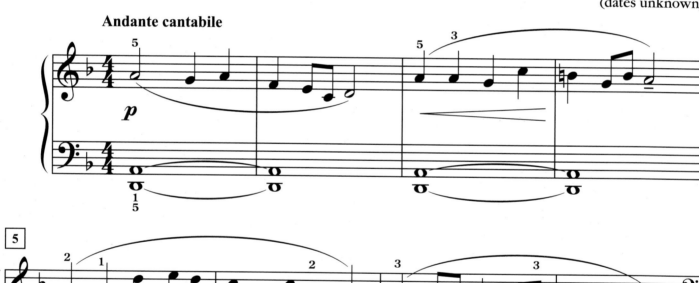

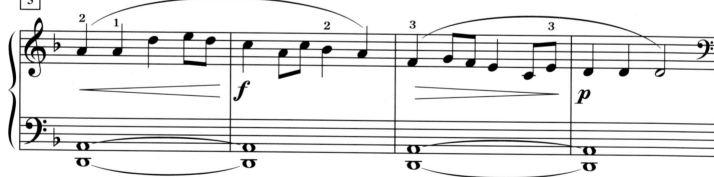

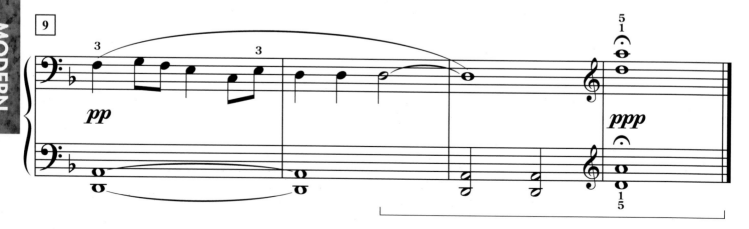

MODERN

Court Dance

Originating in the French Court, **minuets** became the most popular 18th-century dance in European and American ballrooms.

- Minuets were elegant, dignified dances, not too fast since the steps were complicated.

- Facing each other, couples danced to opposite corners of the ballroom, passing each other in the middle where they touched hands.

- The French organist **Jean-Nicolas Geoffroy** composed more than 200 pieces for harpsichord, many of them dances.

Dancing a minuet, from The Art of Dancing *(1735) by Kellom Tomlinson*

Little Minuet

Track 13
⑬ Quick

Allegro moderato

Jean-Nicolas Geoffroy
(1633–1694)

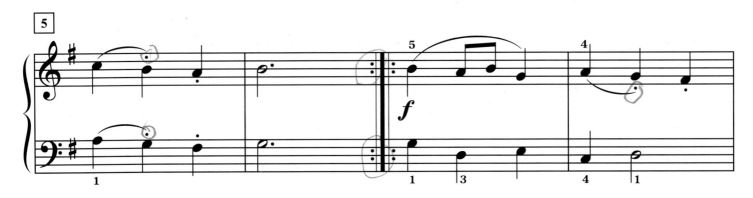

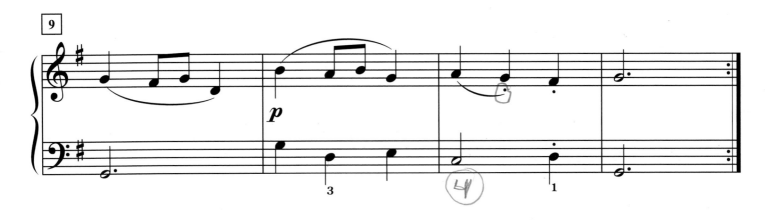

20

Warm-Up Patterns in D Major, p. 22, 24–25, Balancing Melody and Accompaniment, p. 30

BAROQUE

George Frideric Handel

George Frideric Handel is one of the most famous composers of the Baroque era. When he was a child, his father did not want him to study music, so he practiced secretly in the attic of their home.

- When Handel was about 12, a duke heard him play the organ and convinced his father that he should have music lessons.

Handel as a boy

- Although born in Germany, Handel spent the last 50 years of his life in England. **Air** (or ayre) was another word for "song" in 17th-century England.

The house where he was born in Halle, Germany

Track 14

Air

George Frideric Handel
(1685–1759)

Moderato

Ukrainian Folk Dance

Hopak is a folk dance and folk song from the Ukraine. The dancers stamp their heels and perform difficult acrobatic steps in a joyous and enthusiastic way.

Track 15

Hopak

Anonymous

Allegro moderato

MODERN

THE MOZART FAMILY

"My little girl [Nannerl] … only 12 years old is one of the most skillful [keyboard] players in Europe."
—Leopold Mozart

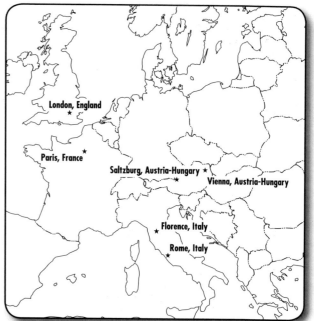

Some of the cities where W. A. Mozart performed as a child

Leopold Mozart was a violinist, conductor, and composer.

- When his daughter Maria Anna (1751-1829), also known as **Nannerl**, was about seven, Leopold compiled the *Notebook for Nannerl,* a book of music to use in her keyboard lessons.

- His son **Wolfgang Amadeus** (1756-1791) was only three but spent hours at the keyboard and was soon playing from Nannerl's notebook, too. By five, Wolfgang was composing minuets, which Leopold added to the notebook.

- In 1761, the entire family traveled from their home in Salzburg to Vienna, Austria, where the children performed for royalty. They soon became famous all over Europe.

- During their concerts, Nannerl and Wolfgang had a trick of playing with the keyboard covered by a cloth so they could not see the keys.

Leopold, Wolfgang, and his sister Nannerl

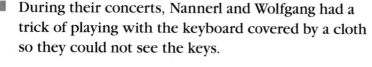

Wolfgang and Nannerl

Mozart's Keyboard Lessons

Leopold Mozart wrote that Wolfgang learned eight minuets (including this one)
when he was four. He learned one in only 30 minutes.

Minuet in F Major

from the *Notebook for Nannerl*

Leopold Mozart
(1719–1787)

CLASSICAL

*Pianists with small hands may omit the top C.

Warm-Up Patterns in G Major, pp. 6–8, Putting Things Together, p. 32

Louis Köhler

Born in what is now Germany, **Louis Köhler** was a respected piano teacher and composer.
By 1914, a book he wrote for teaching piano had sold over 1,000,000 copies. He also compiled
a book of sonatinas that is still used today, over 100 years later.

Andantino
from *Very Easiest Studies*

Louis Köhler (1820–1886)
Op. 190, No. 25

Track 17